Literature Circle Guide:

Holes

by Tonya Ward Singer

SCHOLASTIC
PROFESSIONAL BOOKS

New York • Toronto • London • Auckland • Sydney
• Mexico City • New Delhi • Hong Kong • Buenos Aires

Guide written by Tonya Ward Singer
Edited by Sarah Glasscock
Cover design by Niloufar Safavich
Interior design by Grafica, Inc.
Interior illustrations by Mona Mark

Credits: Cover: Jacket cover for HOLES by Louis Sachar. Copyright © 1998 by Louis Sachar. Reprinted by permission of Farrar, Straus and Giroux, LLC. Interior: Author photo on page 9 by Carla Sachar/Random House. Used by permission.

ISBN 0-439-35538-9

Contents

To the Teacher

As a teacher, you naturally want to instill in your students the habits of confident, critical, independent, and lifelong readers. You hope that even when students are not in school they will seek out books on their own, think about and question what they are reading, and share those ideas with friends. An excellent way to further this goal is by using literature circles in your classroom.

In a literature circle, students select a book to read as a group. They think and write about it on their own in a literature response journal, and then discuss it together. Both journals and discussions enable students to respond to a book and develop their insights into it. They also learn to identify themes and issues, analyze vocabulary, recognize writing techniques, and share ideas with each other—all of which are necessary to meet state and national standards.

This guide provides the support materials for using literature circles with *Holes* by Louis Sachar. The reading strategies, discussion questions, projects, and enrichment readings will also support a whole class reading of this text or can be given to enhance the experience of an individual student reading the book as part of a reading workshop.

Literature Circles

A literature circle consists of several students (usually three to five) who agree to read a book together and share their observations, questions, and interpretations. Groups may be organized by reading level or choice of book. Often these groups read more than one book together since, as students become more comfortable talking with one other, their observations and insights deepen.

When planning to use literature circles in your classroom, it can be helpful to do the following:

❋ Recommend four or five books from which students choose. These books might be grouped by theme, genre, or author.

❋ Allow three or four weeks for students to read each book. Each of Scholastic's *Literature Circle Guides* has the same number of sections as well as enrichment activities and final projects. Even if students are reading different books in the Literature Circle guide series, they can be scheduled to finish at the same time.

❋ Create a daily routine so students can focus on journal writing and discussions.

❋ Decide whether students will be reading books in class or for homework. If students do all their reading for homework, then allot class time for sharing journals and discussions. You can also alternate silent reading and writing days in the classroom with discussion groups.

> ### *Read More About Literature Circles*
>
> *Getting the Most from Literature Groups* by Penny Strube (Scholastic Professional Books, 1996)
>
> *Literature Circles* by Harvey Daniels (Stenhouse Publishers, 1994)

Using the *Literature Circle Guides* in Your Classroom

Each guide contains the following sections:

* background information about the author and book

* enrichment readings relevant to the book

* Literature Response Journal reproducibles

* Group Discussion reproducibles

* Individual and group projects

* Literature Discussion Evaluation Sheet

Background Information and Enrichment Readings

The background information about the author and the book and the enrichment readings are designed to offer information that will enhance students' understanding of the book. You may choose to assign and discuss these sections before, during, or after the reading of the book. Because each enrichment concludes with questions that invite students to connect it to the book, you can use this section to inspire them to think and record their thoughts in the literature response journal.

Literature Response Journal Reproducibles

Although these reproducibles are designed for individual students, they should also be used to stimulate and support discussions in literature circles. Each page begins with a reading strategy and follows with several journal topics. At the bottom of the page, students select a type of response (prediction, question, observation, or connection) for free-choice writing in their response journals.

◆ Reading Strategies

Since the goal of the literature circle is to empower lifelong readers, a different reading strategy is introduced in each section. Not only does the reading strategy allow students to understand this particular book better, it also instills a habit of mind that will continue to be useful when they read other books. A question from the Literature Response Journal and the Group Discussion pages is always tied to the reading strategy.

If everyone in class is reading the same book, you may present the reading strategy as a mini-lesson to the entire class. For literature circles, however, the group of students can read over and discuss the strategy together at the start of class and then experiment with the strategy as they read silently for the rest of the period. You may want to allow time at the end of class so the group can talk about what they noticed as they read. As an alternative, the literature circle can review the reading strategy for the next section after they have completed their discussion. That night, students can try out the reading strategy as they read on their own so they will be ready for the next day's literature circle discussion.

◆ Literature Response Journal Topics

A literature response journal allows a reader to "converse" with a book. Students write questions, point out things they notice about the story, recall personal experiences, and make connections to other texts in their journals. In other words, they are using writing to explore what they think about the book. See page 7 for tips on how to help students set up their literature response journals.

1. The questions for the literature response journals have no right or wrong answers but are designed to help students look beneath the surface of the plot and develop a richer connection to the story and its characters.

2. Students can write in their literature response journals as soon as they have finished a reading assignment. Again, you may choose to have students do this for homework or make time during class.

3. The literature response journals are an excellent tool for students to use in their literature circles. They can highlight ideas and thoughts in their journals that they want to share with the group.

4. When you evaluate students' journals, consider whether they have completed all the assignments and have responded in depth and thoughtfully. You may want to check each day to make sure students are keeping up with the assignments. You can read and respond to the journals at a halfway point (after five entries) and again at the end. Some teachers suggest that students pick out their five best entries for a grade.

Group Discussion Reproducibles

These reproducibles are designed for use in literature circles. Each page begins with a series of discussion questions for the group to consider. A mini-lesson on an aspect of the writer's craft follows the discussion questions. See page 8 for tips on how to model good discussions for students.

◆ **Literature Discussion Questions:** In a literature discussion, students experience a book from different points of view. Each reader brings her or his own unique observations, questions, and associations to the text. When students share their different reading experiences, they often come to a wider and deeper understanding than they would have reached on their own.

The discussion is not an exercise in finding the right answers nor is it a debate. Its goal is to explore the many possible meanings of a book. Be sure to allow enough time for these conversations to move beyond easy answers—try to schedule 25–35 minutes for each one. In addition, there are important guidelines to ensure that everyone's voice is heard.

1. Let students know that participation in the literature discussion is an important part of their grade. You may choose to watch one discussion and grade it. (You can use the Literature Discussion Evaluation Sheet on page 33.)

2. Encourage students to evaluate their own performance in discussions using the Literature Discussion Evaluation Sheet. They can assess not only their own level of involvement but also how the group itself has functioned.

3. Help students learn how to talk to one another effectively. After a discussion, help them process what worked and what didn't. Videotape discussions if possible, and then evaluate them together. Let one literature circle watch another and provide feedback to it.

4. It can be helpful to have a facilitator for each discussion. The facilitator can keep students from interrupting each other, help the conversation get back on track when it digresses, and encourage shyer members to contribute. At the end of each discussion, the facilitator can summarize everyone's contributions and suggest areas for improvement.

5. Designate other roles for group members. For instance, a recorder can take notes and/or list questions for further discussion. A summarizer can open each literature circle meeting by summarizing the chapter(s) the group has just read. Encourage students to rotate these roles, as well as that of the facilitator.

◆ **The Writer's Craft:** This section encourages students to look at the writer's most important tool—words. It points out new vocabulary, writing techniques, and uses of language. One or two questions invite students to think more deeply about the book and writing in general. These questions can either become part of the literature circle discussion or be written about in students' journals.

Literature Discussion Evaluation Sheet

Both you and your students will benefit from completing these evaluation sheets. You can use them to assess students' performance, and as mentioned earlier, students can evaluate their own individual performances, as well as their group's performance. The Literature Discussion Evaluation Sheet appears on page 33.

Setting Up Literature Response Journals

Although some students may already keep literature response journals, others may not know how to begin. To discourage students from merely writing elaborate plot summaries and to encourage them to use their journals in a meaningful way, help them focus their responses around the following elements: predictions, observations, questions, and connections.

Have students take time after each assigned section to think about and record their responses in their journals. Sample responses appear below.

◆ **Predictions:** Before students read the book, have them study the cover and the jacket copy. Ask if anyone has read any other books by Louis Sachar. To begin their literature response journals, tell students to jot down their impressions about the book. As they read, students will continue to make predictions about what a character might do or how the plot might turn. After finishing the book, students can re-assess their initial predictions. Good readers understand that they must constantly activate prior knowledge before, during, and after they read. They adjust their expectations and predictions; a book that is completely predictable is not likely to capture anyone's interest. A student about to read *Holes* for the first time might predict the following:

This book must have something to do with digging holes. From the picture on the cover, it looks like the story takes place on the moon or in the desert. The boy with his cap on backwards is looking sideways like he has something to hide. I bet he did something he wasn't supposed to and is trying not to get caught.

◆ **Observations:** This activity takes place immediately after reading begins. In a literature response journal, the reader recalls fresh impressions about the characters, setting, and events. Most readers mention details that stand out for them even if they are not sure what their importance is. For example, a reader might list phrases that describe how a character looks or the feeling a setting evokes. Many readers note certain words, phrases, or passages in a book. Others note the style of an author's writing or the voice in which the story is told. A student just starting to read *Holes* might write the following:

This place gives me the creeps. Sachar wrote: "The town shriveled and dried up along with the lake and the people who lived there." Now there are only campers digging holes and some mysterious Warden. Weird. As if that isn't bad enough, there are rattlesnakes, scorpions, and deadly yellow spotted lizards to worry about. Forget Camp Green Lake, I'd rather stay home.

◆ **Questions:** Point out that good readers don't necessarily understand everything they read. To clarify their uncertainty, they ask questions. Encourage students to identify passages that confuse or trouble them and emphasize that they shouldn't take anything for granted. Share the following student example:

Who is Stanley Yelnats and why does he have to go to Camp Green Lake? What did he do? Who else has been sent to the camp? How long will they be there? Do kids really get sent away to places like that?

◆ **Connections:** Remind students that one story often leads to another. When one friend tells a story, the other friend is often inspired to tell one too. The same thing happens when someone reads a book. A character reminds the reader of a relative, or a situation is similar to something that happened to him or her. Sometimes a book makes a reader recall other books or movies. These connections can be helpful in revealing some of the deeper meanings or patterns of a book. The following is an example of a student connection:

Stanley's experience in school reminds me of how kids used to tease my best friend, Donna, for being overweight. Donna cried sometimes after school, but never in front of the other kids. She just pretended they didn't bother her. It made me sad. I wonder if anyone was looking out for Stanley at school. He was probably happy to go away.

The Good Discussion

In a good literature discussion, students are always learning from one another. They listen to one another and respond to what their peers have to say. They share their ideas, questions, and observations. Everyone feels comfortable about talking, and no one interrupts or puts down what anyone else says. Students leave a good literature discussion with a new understanding of the book—and sometimes with new questions about it. They almost always feel more engaged by what they have read.

◆ **Modeling a Good Discussion:** In this era of combative and confessional TV talk shows, students often don't have any idea of what it means to talk productively and creatively together. You can help them have a better idea of what a good literature discussion is if you let them experience one. Select a thought-provoking short story or poem for students to read, and then choose a small group to model a discussion of the work for the class.

Explain to participating students that the objective of the discussion is to explore the text thoroughly and learn from one another. Emphasize that it takes time to learn how to have a good discussion, and that the first discussion may not achieve everything they hope it will. Duplicate a copy of the Literature Discussion Evaluation Sheet for each student. Go over the helpful and unhelpful contributions shown on it. Instruct students to fill out the sheet as they watch the model discussion. Then have the group of students hold its discussion while the rest of the class observes. Try not to interrupt or control the discussion and remind the student audience not to participate. It's okay if the discussion falters, as this is a learning experience.

Allow 15–20 minutes for the discussion. When it is finished, ask each student in the group to reflect out loud about what worked and what didn't. Then have the students who observed share their impressions. What kinds of comments were helpful? How could the group have talked to each other more productively? You may want to let another group experiment with a discussion so students can try out what they learned from the first one.

◆ **Assessing Discussions:** The following tips will help students monitor how well their group is functioning:

1. One person should keep track of all behaviors by each group member, both helpful and unhelpful, during the discussion.

2. At the end of the discussion, each individual should think about how he or she did. How many helpful and unhelpful checks did he or she receive?

3. The group should look at the Literature Discussion Evaluation Sheet and assess their performance as a whole. Were most of the behaviors helpful? Were any behaviors unhelpful? How could the group improve?

In good discussions, you will often hear students say the following:

"I was wondering if anyone knew . . ."

"I see what you are saying. That reminds me of something that happened earlier in the book."

"What do you think?"

"Did anyone notice on page 57 that . . ."

"I disagree with you because . . ."

"I agree with you because . . ."

"This reminds me so much of when . . ."

"Do you think this could mean . . ."

"I'm not sure I understand what you're saying. Could you explain it a little more to me?"

"That reminds me of what you were saying yesterday about . . ."

"I just don't understand this."

"I love the part that says . . ."

"Here, let me read this paragraph. It's an example of what I'm talking about."

About *Holes*

Secrets and venomous lizards hide in the shadows of Camp Green Lake, a correctional facility for "bad boys." Once you begin reading about the characters in this desolate place, you'll find it hard to stop. *Holes* unravels mysteries of past and future through a realistic tale of adventure and suspense.

It has won numerous awards including the Newbery Medal, the National Book Award, and The New York Times Outstanding Book of the Year. Of all the books author Louis Sachar has written, *Holes* is his favorite.

About the Author: Louis Sachar

Louis Sachar did not always know he would become an author. While working as a noon supervisor at an elementary school near his college, he became inspired to write about the adventures of different kids. Sachar began to write stories as a hobby without expecting to become published, but the stories became his first book *Sideways Stories from Wayside School*.

Even after his first published success, Sachar was uncertain about whether to become an author or a lawyer. He completed law school and became an attorney, while writing on his own time. After publishing three more children's books, Sachar realized he wanted to devote all his time to writing.

As Sachar reveals in the following quote, when he began writing *Holes*, he wanted to write something completely different from his previous books:

"It was August, and the weather was hot, and I got the idea to write about a juvenile correctional facility, a boot camp for 'bad boys,' where they were required to dig holes, every day, under the brutal Texas sun. Thus, I created Camp Green Lake, where there was no lake, and hardly anything was green.

"I didn't know what was going to happen there, or even who the main character would be. But I threw in some buried treasure, and deadly yellow spotted lizards, and the place seemed ripe for a story. Lots of different stories could have grown out of that place."

Sachar is currently writing a screenplay for *Holes* and hopes it will become a movie. He also would like to write another book that excites him as much as *Holes*. Sachar has the following advice for young authors:

"Read, find out what you like to read, and try to figure out what it is about it that makes you like it. And you have to rewrite. My first draft of anything I write is really awful. "

Other Books by Louis Sachar

Dogs Don't Tell Jokes

More Sideways Arithmetic from Wayside School

Sideways Arithmetic from Wayside School

Sideways Stories from Wayside School

Stories from Wayside School

Super Fast, Out of Control!

There's a Boy in the Girls' Bathroom

Wayside School Gets a Little Stranger

Wayside School Is Falling Down

Why Pick on Me?

Enrichment: Juvenile Justice

Since the mid-1980s, military-style boot camps have become a common form of punishment for juvenile offenders in the United States. There are currently an estimated 4,000 children in approximately 50 camps nationwide. Programs vary, but many have the tough-love philosophy that kids must be broken down before they can be built up again.

"Nobody can tell me from some ivory tower that you take a kid, kick him in the rear end, and it doesn't do him any good," said former governor Zell Miller of Georgia, who was an early proponent of juvenile boot camps.

This attitude has lead to abuse in some cases. At least six children have died in detention, and hundreds more have been subjected to physical and emotional abuse. Over the past two decades, the Youth Law Center has filed lawsuits against juvenile facilities in 19 states. Some guards and corrections officials have been fired or prosecuted, and camps have been closed down or forced to change their programs.

While juvenile boot camps have been criticized for being too harsh, they may be an improvement over past methods of juvenile reform. In seventeenth-century England, children were sent to prison for committing crimes as minor as stealing a loaf of bread. They were mixed in with the general adult population of criminals and didn't receive any special treatment or care.

A century later, English children who committed minor crimes were shipped to Australian prison colonies with hard-core adult criminals.

American children were tried as adults until July 1899 when the Illinois Juvenile Court Act set a precedent for other states by establishing distinct courts for juvenile offenders. The new system focused more on rehabilitation than punishment and on placing children in separate facilities from adults.

Today's juvenile justice system is overloaded by over a million cases each year. Judges have limited time to review each case and thus can make quick decisions based on limited information. Two-thirds of all cases are dismissed or return the juvenile to the custody of his or her parents or guardians. Sentencing for the remaining cases is limited to the options provided by each state, which might include juvenile detention, counseling, drug rehabilitation, adult incarceration, or juvenile boot camps.

There is still considerable debate in our society about how we should treat young people who commit crimes. Some insist that punishment should be a first priority, while others argue that rehabilitation is a better way to prevent children from committing crimes in the future. As you read, think about Stanley's experience with the justice system. Is it realistic? Is it fair? Do you think it would be possible for some kids to benefit from a program like Camp Green Lake?

Enrichment: Gila Monsters

Although the yellow spotted lizard feared in *Holes* is fictional, it's not far from the truth. It resembles the Gila monster, one of two venomous lizards in the world today.

Gila monsters live in the dry habitats of the southwestern United States. They are much larger than an average lizard with stout bodies that can grow up to 56 cm long. They have heavy claws and short tails and are recognizable by colorful scale designs of black on a yellow, orange, or pink background.

Since their strong jaws are sufficient to capture prey, Gila monsters rarely use their venom when hunting for food. They eat turtle eggs, small lizards, rabbits, rodents and snakes. In one meal, a young Gila monster can eat the equivalent of half of its body weight. Imagine how much food that would be for a human: Take your body weight and divide it in half. That's how many pounds of food you would eat at one sitting if you consumed as much food as a Gila monster!

Luckily Gila monsters don't eat three meals a day. Their slow metabolism allows them to digest food over a long period of time. One adult can live for a year on three to four good meals.

Gila monsters are hard to find because they spend most of the year undercover. Between November and March, they hibernate in underground burrows. Even during the months they are active, Gila monsters spend most of their time in shelters. They may be above ground for a total of only 190 hours during the entire year, or two percent of their lives.

If you're lucky enough to see a Gila monster, keep your distance, and it should leave you alone. Gila monsters are more interested in finding food and protecting themselves than in biting humans. They are not aggressive unless provoked. If a Gila monster feels threatened, it will try to back away and hide. If it is unable to retreat, the lizard will hiss and open its mouth to threaten the attacker. As a last resort, it will lunge and bite.

The Gila monster does not strike like a snake; instead, it bites firmly and hangs on with a tight grip to "chew" in the venom. While Gila monster bites are rare, they can be deadly. In one case, a victim died in 52 minutes after being bitten. This is the exception—most humans survive the bite of a Gila monster.

Humans are more of a threat to Gila monsters than the reverse. In the past, people shot the lizards on sight or intentionally ran over them in cars. Now Gila monsters are legally protected in this country from hunting and capture. They are threatened, however, by human pollution and changes to their natural habitat.

As you read about yellow spotted lizards in the book, try to separate fact from fiction. How are the lizards like real Gila monsters? How are they different?

Enrichment:
Women of the Wild West

Western outlaws and bandits in the late 1800s inspired a name for their place in history: the Wild West. It is difficult to know the whole truth about these characters because writers of the time often exaggerated the details of the outlaws' lives. They described poker games in dusty salons, gunfights, and stagecoach robberies, blurring fiction and fact to transform real people and events into exciting reading.

Popular "dime novels," widely read and sold from 1860 until 1910, portrayed real Western characters as larger-than-life folk heroes. These tall tales glamorized the lives of outlaws such as Billy the Kid and Jesse James. While these men were among the most famous outlaws, they were not alone. Several women became well-known sharp shooters and bandits of the Wild West.

Phoebe Anne Moss earned her reputation as an expert with a shotgun and a rifle. She became known as "Annie Oakley," a sharp-shooter in Buffalo Bill's Wild West Show. Oakley could shoot a dime flipped in the air or shatter a playing card held sideways at 30 paces. Rumor has it that she could even shoot a cigarette out of her husband's mouth!

Martha Jane Cannary became known as "Calamity Jane" because she was trouble to any man who crossed her path. It was said she could shoot, drink, and swear as well as any man in the West. Calamity Jane invented details of her life, making it difficult to separate fact from fiction. In truth, she never was an outlaw, but a character to remember.

Myra Belle Starr, "the Bandit Queen," wore a black velvet skirt and black riding cap with a large ostrich feather covering her face. On her hip, she wore her "baby"—a Colt .45 pistol. Belle first became an outlaw by fleeing to California with a fugitive, her husband Jim Reed. Years after lawmen shot Reed, Belle married Sam Starr. Together they settled in Younger's Bend, a home that became their hideout as well as a refuge for other traveling outlaws. In the early 1880s, Belle was known to steal horses from surrounding ranches and towns.

She took pride in preserving some of the ladylike manners expected of women in that time. Belle played piano and never smoked cigars. One day her hat blew off when she was riding near Fort Smith. When a cowboy who saw the incident refused to chase the hat, Belle drew her Colt .45 and ordered him to pick it up. He did. Belle put her hat on her head and said, "The next time a lady asks you to pick up her hat, do as she tells you."

As with most outlaws of the Wild West, Belle Starr's reputation is an exaggeration of the truth. Some reports say she dressed as a man to help rob a stagecoach of $30,000 in gold. Others claim she led an outlaw gang and would shoot a man down as soon as look at him. While Starr used her gun to threaten people, she never did pull the trigger.

As you read *Holes*, compare Kissin' Kate Barlow the bandit to Katherine Barlow the teacher. Is there a difference between Barlow's true character and the outlaw she was reputed to be?

Name _____ Date _____

Holes
Before Reading the Book

Reading Strategy: Using Prior Knowledge

Your understanding of a new book begins even before you read the first page. Your knowledge and life experiences can help you imagine and understand the setting, characters, and events in a story. Think about the title and pictures on the cover of *Holes*. Read the information on the book jacket. What are your first responses to the book?

Writing in Your Literature Response Journal

A. Write about one of these topics in your journal. Circle the topic you chose.

1. Think about the title. What do you know about holes? A hole can be visible, or something invisible such as a hole in a story. Make a list of possible types of holes. How do you expect holes to relate to this novel?

2. Have you ever moved, changed schools, or traveled to an unfamiliar place on your own? Describe your experiences. What were your expectations and first impressions? How did they change over time?

3. What do you know about your great-great-grandparents and your other ancestors who lived before you? Write about one of your ancestors. Include what you know about this person as well as questions you have. What connections can you find between your ancestor's life and your own?

B. What were your predictions, questions, observations, and connections about the book? Write about one of them in your journal. Check the response you chose.

❏ Prediction   ❏ Question   ❏ Observation   ❏ Connection

Literature Circle Guide for *Holes* • Scholastic Professional Books

Name _____ **Date** _____

Holes

Before Reading the Book

For Your Discussion Group

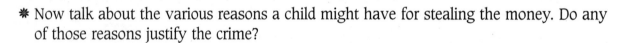

✳ Discuss what you already know about juvenile justice. What happens to a child who is caught breaking the law? What do the police do? What rights does the child have?

✳ Imagine the police catch a twelve-year-old who has stolen $100 from a store. Should the theft be punished, and if so, how? Take turns letting each person in the group be the judge and determining a fair consequence. After each person has passed judgment, discuss the possible impact each consequence might have on a child.

✳ Now talk about the various reasons a child might have for stealing the money. Do any of those reasons justify the crime?

✳ What questions do you still have about juvenile justice in the United States? Brainstorm a list of questions that remain unanswered for your group. Think about which people and resources in your community can help you find the answers. Form pairs, choose questions, and become detectives to seek out the answers before your next meeting.

TIP

When you are brainstorming, remember that the goal is to collect as many different ideas as possible without commenting on them. Everybody's ideas should be included.

Literature Circle Guide for *Holes* • Scholastic Professional Books

Name _____ **Date** _____

Holes

Chapters 1–6

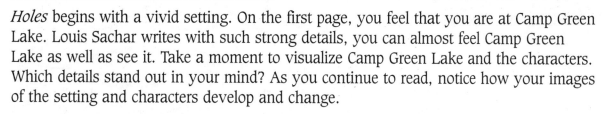

Reading Strategy: Visualizing

Holes begins with a vivid setting. On the first page, you feel that you are at Camp Green Lake. Louis Sachar writes with such strong details, you can almost feel Camp Green Lake as well as see it. Take a moment to visualize Camp Green Lake and the characters. Which details stand out in your mind? As you continue to read, notice how your images of the setting and characters develop and change.

Writing in Your Literature Response Journal

A. **Write about one of these topics in your journal. Circle the topic you chose.**

1. Visualize Stanley's trip to and arrival at Camp Green Lake. What does he see? What does he smell and feel? What do you think he might hear and taste? Write your own description of the setting.

2. Have you ever been punished for something you did not do? Did you accept the punishment or resist? Write about your actions.

3. How did Stanley react to his conviction? What do you learn about his character from his reaction?

4. Have you ever been bullied or teased by other kids? What did you do about it? Do you think you have ever been a bully? Describe one experience and how it influenced you or other people.

B. **What were your predictions, questions, observations, and connections as you read? Write about one of them in your journal. Check the response you chose.**

❏ Prediction ❏ Question ❏ Observation ❏ Connection

Literature Circle Guide for *Holes* • Scholastic Professional Books

Name _____ **Date** _____

Holes

Chapters 1–6

For Your Discussion Group

✳ Read the following quote from the book:

If you take a bad boy and make him dig a hole every day in the hot sun, it will turn him into a good boy.

That was what some people thought.

Do you agree with the quote? Will digging holes every day change a boy's character? Discuss whether digging holes is a fair punishment. Do you think the author agrees with you? Explain your reasons.

✳ If you were given the choice between Camp Green Lake and jail, which one would you choose, and why? If Stanley had known what Camp Green Lake was really like, do you think he would have made the same decision?

✳ Stanley's father believes that people learn from failure. Do you agree or disagree with him? Give an example to support your view.

Writer's Craft: Atmosphere

The campers are forbidden to lie in the hammock. It belongs to the Warden. The Warden owns the shade.

There is a strange tension in the air in the very first chapter. Louis Sachar immediately lays out the **atmosphere** of Camp Green Lake, or the mood and emotion of the setting. He creates such a strong atmosphere through his descriptions that you feel the mood and unspoken rules of Camp Green Lake. Which words and sentences in the first two chapters give you the strongest sense of atmosphere?

Literature Circle Guide for *Holes* • Scholastic Professional Books

Name _____   **Date** _____

Holes
Chapters 7–12

Reading Strategy: Summarizing

To keep track of the characters and events in a story, it is
helpful to stop and summarize what you have already
read. This will help you remember important events and identify any confusion you may
have. Briefly summarize Stanley's experience so far. If you are uncertain about any key
events or characters, skim the previous chapters and reread any sections to help clarify
your understanding.

Writing in Your Literature Response Journal

A. **Write about one of these topics in your journal. Circle the topic you chose.**

  1. Summarize Stanley's story of his great-great-grandfather, Elya Yelnats. What
  relevance do you think Elya's experiences have to Stanley's life now? What's
  your opinion of the story?

  2. All the boys at Camp Green Lake have nicknames. Do you have a nickname? If
  so, do you like it? What are the advantages of having a nickname? How do you
  think Caveman, Zero, and X-Ray feel about their nicknames?

  3. Why does Stanley make Camp Green Lake seem like a real camp in his letter to
  his mom? Imagine that you were a camper at Camp Green Lake. Write a letter
  home to your family or a friend.

B. **What were your predictions, questions, observations, and connections as you
read? Write about one of them in your journal. Check the response you chose.**

❑ Prediction   ❑ Question   ❑ Observation   ❑ Connection

Literature Circle Guide for Holes • Scholastic Professional Books

Name _____ **Date** _____

Holes
Chapters 7–12

For Your Discussion Group

❋ Have each person in your group
select a character from Camp Green
Lake to describe. Take turns briefly
summarizing what you know about
each character. Ask one another
any questions you have about
the characters.

❋ Take turns sharing your goals for the future. Do you agree with Mr. Pendanski that
everyone must have goals in order to stay out of trouble?

❋ Is Stanley really cursed because of his "no-good-dirty-rotten-pig-stealing-great-great-
grandfather," or is that just a family joke? Do you believe in the power of curses?

Writer's Craft: Interweaving Stories

In this book, Louis Sachar weaves his narration between the past and the present. In
Chapter 7, he describes Stanley digging his first hole, and he also tells the story of Elya
Yelnats. Not only does the time period change, but the point of view also changes.
Sachar shifts from the present and Stanley's voice to the past and Elya's voice. Instead
of telling the story in chronological order, the author reveals information about the past
in bits and pieces. The extra space inserted between the paragraphs indicates when the
story changes.

As you read, observe how Sachar continues to link the past and present. Would you
prefer to have the events of the story told in the order in which they happened? Why do
you think Sachar chose to write the book in this way?

Literature Circle Guide for *Holes* • Scholastic Professional Books

Name _____ Date _____

Holes
Chapters 13–18

Reading Strategy: Making Predictions

Any reader of *Holes* is bound to be curious by now. What will become of Stanley and the rest of the boys at Camp Green Lake? What will the Warden do next? Will Zero find a teacher? Each time a turn in the story leaves you wondering about the future, make a prediction about what might happen. Adjust your predictions as you read.

Writing in Your Literature Response Journal

A. Write about one of these topics in your journal. Circle the topic you chose.

1. What do you think the Warden hopes to find? Do you think she'll be successful? Predict the outcome of all this digging.

2. What is the gold tube Stanley found? What do you think the initials KB mean? What kind of connection might this gold tube have to the past?

3. Describe your earliest memories of learning to read. How would your life be different now if you did not know how to read this sentence? Explain whether you think it's easier to teach someone to read than to learn to read.

B. What were your predictions, questions, observations, and connections as you read? Write about one of them in your journal. Check the response you chose.

❑ Prediction   ❑ Question   ❑ Observation   ❑ Connection

Literature Circle Guide for *Holes* • Scholastic Professional Books

Name _____ **Date** _____

Holes
Chapters 13–18

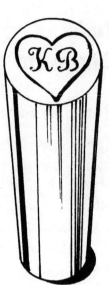

For Your Discussion Group

✱ Take turns sharing your predictions about what will happen next in the story. Which clues in the text informed your predictions?

✱ Who is the Warden? Describe her personality and appearance. How does she control Mr. Sir and Mr. Pendanski? Is it effective? Imagine if she were your substitute teacher for a day. What would she do?

Writer's Craft: Character Development

Good dialogue involves the reader in both the spoken and unspoken parts of a conversation. Feel the tension in the following exchange between the Warden and Mr. Pendanski:

"I just filled them a little while ago," said Mr. Pendanski.

The Warden stared hard at him. "Excuse me," she said. Her voice was soft.

"I had just filled them when Rex—"

"Excuse me," the Warden said again. "Did I ask you when you last filled them?"

"No, but it's just—"

"Excuse me."

Mr. Pendanski stopped talking. The Warden wiggled her finger for him to come to her.

What is not being said? What does this conversation tell you about the characters?

Notice how Louis Sachar includes interruptions, repetition, and pauses in the dialogue. Are these elements of real conversations? Listen to people talking around you to find out. Write some examples of real-life dialogues in your journal.

Literature Circle Guide for *Holes* • Scholastic Professional Books

Name _____ **Date** _____

Holes

Chapters 19–24

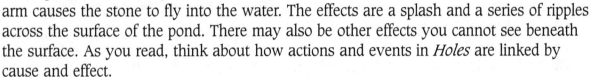

Reading Strategy: Recognizing Cause and Effect

Events in life and in fiction are often linked by cause and effect. Imagine you throw a stone into a pond. The action you create with your arm causes the stone to fly into the water. The effects are a splash and a series of ripples across the surface of the pond. There may also be other effects you cannot see beneath the surface. As you read, think about how actions and events in *Holes* are linked by cause and effect.

Writing in Your Literature Response Journal

A. **Write about one of these topics in your journal. Circle the topic you chose.**

1. Notice how Stanley's lie about stealing the sunflower seeds causes a chain of events which comes back to affect his life at the camp. List what happens as a result of his lie. Notice how each character's action affects the other characters and their actions. How do you think things would have changed if Stanley hadn't lied?

2. Have you ever lied to protect someone else? Did it work? Are there any situations in which lying can be a good thing? Offer several examples to justify your opinion.

3. What was your response when the Warden scratched Mr. Sir's face? Did her actions change your view of her? Explain whether you think Mr. Sir will seek revenge on the Warden—or has he learned his lesson?

B. **What were your predictions, questions, observations, and connections as you read? Write about one of them in your journal. Check the response you chose.**

❑ Prediction   ❑ Question   ❑ Observation   ❑ Connection

Literature Circle Guide for *Holes* • Scholastic Professional Books

Name _____   Date _____

Holes
Chapters 19–24

For Your Discussion Group

✳ Why do you think Stanley lied
about the sunflower seeds? Take
turns telling what you would have
done in the same situation.

✳ What agreement did Stanley and
Zero make? What do you think caused Stanley to change his mind about helping
Zero? Tell whether you think the deal is fair. How do you expect the other characters
at Camp Green Lake to react to this arrangement?

✳ Who is KB? What do you know about her?

Writer's Craft: Metaphors and Similes

The following sentence from *Holes* has a double meaning:

> *The rattlesnake would be a lot more dangerous if it didn't have a rattle.*

On the surface, the sentence is about a rattlesnake that literally shook the rattle on its
tail. But it can also be interpreted as a metaphor about another warning that Stanley
received. A **metaphor** is a comparison in which one object is used to represent someone
or something else. Who or what is the rattlesnake in Stanley's life? How was Stanley
warned?

Similes are comparisons that are introduced by the words *as* or *like*. In Chapter 24,
Louis Sachar describes Stanley's thirst in the following way:

> *His mouth was as dry and as parched as the lake.*

Think of similes to describe how hot, tired, thirsty, lonely, or hungry Stanley was after a
hard day of digging holes.

Literature Circle Guide for *Holes* • Scholastic Professional Books

Name _____ **Date** _____

Holes
Chapters 25–30

Reading Strategy: Focusing on Important Details

There are many clues in *Holes* to help you make
connections between different parts of the story. Details
that seem minor at first become central to your
understanding of how separate scenes tie together.
Names, physical descriptions, and objects reveal
connections between the present and the past. As you read about the town of Green
Lake 110 years ago, look for details that link that history to present events and
characters at Camp Green Lake. Record the details and connections in your journal.

Writing in Your Literature Response Journal

A. **Write about one of these topics in your journal. Circle the topic you chose.**

1. Search for important details in Chapter 28. Which clues reveal connections
between the past and present? How does Linda Walker relate to the rest of the
story? What does this one scene involving her tell you about the history of Camp
Green Lake?

2. Have you experienced discrimination for being different? What happened? What
did you do?

3. What is Zero's real name? What does that name tell you about his history? Use
this information to make predictions about his future.

B. **What were your predictions, questions, observations, and connections as you
read? Write about one of them in your journal. Check the response you chose.**

❑ Prediction ❑ Question ❑ Observation ❑ Connection

Literature Circle Guide for *Holes* • Scholastic Professional Books

Name _____   Date _____

Holes
Chapters 25–30

For Your Discussion Group

✸ Which details reveal the racial problems in the town of Green Lake? Discuss what you know about race relations in the United States in the 1880s and 1890s. How long had slavery been abolished? What major historical events have happened since that time that have had an impact on race relations in this country?

✸ Does racism exist among the boys at Camp Green Lake? How do you know?

✸ After describing the town's reaction to Katherine Barlow kissing Sam, Sachar wrote the following:

That all happened one hundred and ten years ago. Since then, not one drop of rain has fallen on Green Lake.

You make the decision: Whom did God punish?

Why do you think the author asked this question? How do you think he would answer it? What would your answer be?

Writer's Craft: Names

Louis Sachar uses names in a variety of ways in this book. Some names reveal specific information about the characters they represent, such as the nicknames of boys at Camp Green Lake. What do the names X-Ray, Caveman, and Zero reveal about each character? What problem does Trout Walker's name expose? Even names without literal meanings reflect their characters. What does the Warden's use of her title rather than her name tell you about her personality? What impression do you get from the name Mr. Sir? Other names in *Holes* reveal connections between characters and their ancestors. How do Stanley's and Zero's names link them to their past?

Literature Circle Guide for *Holes* • Scholastic Professional Books

Name _____ **Date** _____

Holes
Chapters 31–37

Reading Strategy: Making Connections

Good readers naturally make connections between
their own lives and the stories they read. Even if you have never been to a place like
Camp Green Lake, you may have experienced the same feelings or faced similar
challenges as the characters in the book. Examining these connections can help you
understand the characters and their actions on a deeper level. Which situations or events
in the story remind you of your own experiences?

Writing in Your Literature Response Journal

A. **Write about one of these topics in your journal. Circle the topic you chose.**

1. Think about the challenges Stanley and Zero face as they climb God's Thumb.
Have you ever tried to do something extremely difficult? Write about the experience. How were your struggles similar to Stanley and Zero's?

2. What does the word *hope* mean to you? Why is hope important to Stanley and
Zero? What gives them hope? How do they create it for themselves?

3. Do any of the characters remind you of someone in your own life? Compare a
person you know to a character in the book. How are they similar? How are
they different?

B. **What were your predictions, questions, observations, and connections as you**
read? Write about one of them in your journal. Check the response you chose.

❏ Prediction ❏ Question ❏ Observation ❏ Connection

Literature Circle Guide for *Holes* • Scholastic Professional Books

Name _____   **Date** _____

Holes
Chapters 31–37

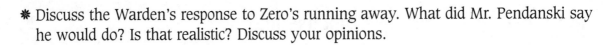

For Your Discussion Group

✳ Take turns having each member of the group share one connection between the story and his or her own life. Think about similar situations you have experienced or a time you felt like one of the characters felt in the story. How do your experiences help you understand the characters and their actions?

✳ Discuss the Warden's response to Zero's running away. What did Mr. Pendanski say he would do? Is that realistic? Discuss your opinions.

✳ What risks did Stanley take in going after Zero? Talk about what else he could have done to help his friend. What would you have done if you were in Stanley's shoes when Zero ran away?

Writer's Craft: Suspense

As the sentence below illustrates, Louis Sachar leaves his readers hanging at the end of many chapters.

Then a dark hand and an orange sleeve reached up and out of the tunnel.

The sentence gives readers a taste of what to expect later in the story without giving it away. This is the key to suspenseful writing: Reveal just enough information to keep the reader guessing and turning pages.

Do you ever find it difficult to stop reading this book? Which points in the story have been especially suspenseful? What makes them so suspenseful? Notice what information is revealed and what is left out.

Literature Circle Guide for *Holes* • Scholastic Professional Books

Name _____ **Date** _____

Holes
Chapters 38–43

Reading Strategy: Compare and Contrast

Since the beginning of *Holes*, you have followed the adventures of characters in the present as well as those who lived over a hundred years ago. You have kept track of events in Camp Green Lake, the former town of Green Lake, and in the lives of Stanley's ancestors. Many of the links between each time and place are subtle—or are yet to be revealed. To find connections among the different parts of the plot, compare and contrast two events, places, or characters from different points in time. How are they the same? How are they different?

Writing in Your Literature Response Journal

A. **Write about one of these topics in your journal. Circle the topic you chose.**

1. Stanley sings a familiar song to Zero. Who else do you remember singing that song? What meaning did it have? Compare and contrast the different times the song was sung to look for similarities in the scenes. What connections can you find?

2. Have you ever confessed to doing something wrong? How did others react? Did your confession make things better or worse? Compare your experience to Zero's.

3. Stanley wants to dig one more hole. What does he hope to find? Make a prediction about what will happen at the end of the story.

B. **What were your predictions, questions, observations, and connections as you read? Write about one of them in your journal. Check the response you chose.**

❏ Prediction   ❏ Question   ❏ Observation   ❏ Connection

Literature Circle Guide for *Holes* • Scholastic Professional Books

Name _____   **Date** _____

Holes

Chapters 38–43

For Your Discussion Group

The following quote reveals Stanley's thoughts about himself:

It occurred to him that he couldn't remember the last time he felt happiness. It wasn't just being sent to Camp Green Lake that had made his life miserable. Before that he'd been unhappy at school, where he had no friends, and bullies like Derrick Dunne picked on him. No one liked him, and the truth was, he didn't especially like himself. He liked himself now.

✽ Compare Stanley's character now to who he was before coming to Camp Green Lake. How has he changed? How has his experience at the camp contributed to that change? Explain whether you would be happy in Stanley's situation.

✽ Brainstorm a list of all the connections you can find between Stanley's family history, the old town of Green Lake, and the present adventures of Stanley and Zero. Write your ideas on a large piece of paper. What has carried over from past to present? Which characters are connected? How do you know? Save your list for your next discussion.

Writer's Craft: Sounds of Language

Read the sentence below out loud and listen to the sounds in the words.

The ground became gloppier. The mud splashed up as he slapped the ground.

The language has the same fluid quality as the mud it describes. Sachar accomplishes this by writing with alliteration, assonance, and onomatopoeia. Notice the repetition of sounds within the two sentences. **Alliteration** is the repetition of the initial sounds of words, for example, *ground* and *gloppier*. **Assonance** is the repetition of vowel sounds within a sentence. Which vowel sounds are repeated in the sentences? The words *slap* and *glop* are **onomatopoetic**—they sound like the meanings they represent. The words mimic the sounds of a person crawling through mud. Reread the paragraphs about Stanley and Zero discovering mud. What other examples of alliteration, assonance, or onomatopoeia can you find?

Literature Circle Guide for *Holes* • Scholastic Professional Books

Name _____   **Date** _____

Holes
Chapters 44–50

Reading Strategy: Asking Questions

Asking questions is a powerful way for readers to engage in a story. As you read the final chapters, your curiosity about how *Holes* will end is probably building. What do you still want to know about the characters and events? Are your questions answered by the end of the book? After you finish the book, look through your journal for questions you had as you were reading. Were all your questions answered?

Writing in Your Literature Response Journal

A. Write about one of these topics in your journal. Circle the topic you chose.

1. The story ends with some holes left for you to fill with your imagination. What questions do you still have about the lives of Stanley, Zero, and the characters at Camp Green Lake? Write your questions in your journal, and then answer them as you think Louis Sachar might.

2. Who is singing to Hector Zeroni at the end of the story? What questions do you think Hector will ask her? How do you think she will respond? What questions do you have about their future together?

3. Why did Stanley's luck change? Why did rain fall on Green Lake for the first time in over a hundred years? Was it due to the breaking of a curse or was it just coincidence? Explain your perspective.

B. What were your predictions, questions, observations, and connections as you read? Write about one of them in your journal. Check the response you chose.

❏ Prediction   ❏ Question   ❏ Observation   ❏ Connection

Literature Circle Guide for *Holes* • Scholastic Professional Books

Name _____ Date _____

Holes

Chapters 44–50

For Your Discussion Group

✳ Reread the list of connections you
wrote during your last discussion.
Now that you have finished the
book, are there any changes you
need to make to your list? Add any
new connections you have
discovered. How do those
connections clarify your
understanding of people
and events in the story?

✳ Ask one another any questions you still have about the lives of the characters in
Holes. What do you still want to know about the past? What do you want to know
about the future? Take turns asking your questions to one another and discussing
possible answers.

Writer's Craft: Conflict

*Stanley felt tiny claws dig into the side of his face as the lizard pulled itself off his
neck and up past his chin.*

"It won't be long now," the Warden said.

Conflict is what makes a story interesting. It is the essence of plot. Conflict creates
tension and lures us to read on to find out how the problem will be resolved. Imagine
how the final scene at Camp Green Lake would have been different if Stanley and Zero
had discovered the wooden suitcase without any problems. Think about the conflicts
they encountered. What conflicts existed for the Warden and Mr. Sir? How were these
resolved? Were any major conflicts left unresolved at the end of the book?

Literature Circle Guide for *Holes* • Scholastic Professional Books

Holes
After Reading

Many stories contain a **moral**. A **moral** is a lesson or principal that is taught in a story or event. Since a novel is composed of many events, multiple morals can be embedded within the different turns of the plot. Some morals are clearly defined, while others are subtle and left open to the interpretation of each reader.

✻ Think about the lessons that can be learned from the experiences of the characters in *Holes*. What messages has Louis Sachar communicated through his book?

✻ In life as well as fiction, conflict and struggle are powerful teachers. They can also help pinpoint the morals in a story. Reflect on one conflict or problem in *Holes*. Discover the moral behind the conflict by looking at how it is resolved in the book.

✻ Create this simple chart in your literature response journal to organize your thoughts. Divide one page into three columns. Write the following column headings: Conflict/Problem, Resolution/Consequences, Moral(s).

✻ In the first column, summarize the problem or conflict from the story. In the second column, write about how the problem is resolved or unresolved. Include any related consequences for the characters or plot. Use the third column to write your interpretation of the moral. Remember, there are many possible interpretations for each situation. Study the example below, but write your own interpretation.

Conflict/Problem	Resolution/Consequences	Moral(s)
Katherine Barlow and Sam cared for each other, but the townspeople thought it was wrong for a white woman and black man to kiss.	Katherine Barlow kissed Sam. People in Green Lake shot Sam and his mule Mary Lou. Kate Barlow became an outlaw. Rain stopped falling on Green Lake.	1. Racism is harmful. 2. What goes around, comes around. People who are cruel will be punished in some way.

✻ Discuss your ideas in your group. Which morals do you think are most important to the author? Which are most important to you?

Literature Circle Guide for *Holes* • Scholastic Professional Books

Individual Projects

1. Imagine you are Stanley and have the opportunity to write a letter back in time. Write to your great-great-grandfather Elya Yelnats and describe the influence he has had on your life. What do you want to tell him about the future? What do you want to know about his past?

2. Draw a map of present-day Camp Green Lake and the surrounding area. Place a clean transparency over your map and tape it to the paper on one side. On the transparency, revise the map to show the town of Green Lake as it may have looked over 110 years ago. Trace any buildings and natural landmarks that are the same on both maps. Add any details that are different.

3. After you read the final page of *Holes*, did you wonder about what would happen next in the lives of any characters? This is your chance to answer your questions. Write chapter 51, and tell what becomes of Zero, Stanley, the Warden, or any other characters you want to involve.

- -

Group Projects

1. *Holes* is an exciting story for the stage or screen. Select one of your favorite scenes from the book to perform before your class. Adapt the scene by adding or revising lines as necessary to make it work as a classroom play. Memorize your lines, create actions for the characters, and rehearse before the show. If you have access to a video camera, film your scene so you can share it with different classes, friends, and family.

2. Learn more about juvenile justice in your state. Talk with local police officers and do research at the library and on the Internet for information about how kids are treated for breaking the law. What are the possible punishments for a child caught stealing? Present your findings on a bulletin board that includes both information about the current system and your opinions on how it should be changed.

3. Create a board game based on *Holes*. Discuss which events and characters are most essential to the novel and include them in your design. How will you incorporate the past and present stories of Green Lake? What elements of the plot will you choose to omit? When you complete your game, try it out. After making any necessary revisions, teach the game to other students in your class.

Literature Circle Guide for *Holes* • Scholastic Professional Books